Great eBay Photos - The Easy Way!

Techniques Anyone Can Use!

Judy Wesener

Disclaimer

No part of this book may be reproduced in any form without written permission for the author, with the exception of very brief excerpts used in the writing of reviews.

Neither the author nor the publisher assumes any responsibility for any errors, omissions, or contrary interpretations of this subject matter.

This book is intended for general information. Views expressed are those of the author alone, and are not intended as expert instruction, or as guidance or diagnosis of any condition or problem.

Neither the author nor the publisher assumes any responsibility or liability whatsoever on behalf of the purchaser or reader of this book. Adherence to all applicable laws and regulations, including international, federal, state, provincial and local, in Canada, Great Britain, the United States and all other countries is the sole responsibility of the purchaser or reader.

Judy Wesener

"If your pictures aren't good enough,
you're not close enough."

-Robert Capa

Judy Wesener

CONTENTS

Preface

Remember, this is not a book on how to become a professional photographer. It was written to give you straightforward, easy to understand, instructions on how to quickly and easily take photos you can use for your online sales.

The methods here will work for you, whether you're selling on eBay, Amazon, your own website or any other online site.

Always keep in mind that a good picture can make the difference between your item selling or just sitting there for who knows how long. In fact, it may never sell. Contrary to popular belief, not everything sells, but that's a whole different topic.

Spending extra time on your photos will always be in your best interest. This is time well invested and will pay off in the end.

Listing without pictures, or with bad pictures, quite honestly, is really not a good idea. You won't get the volume of traffic that a listing with a good photo will receive. Think of it from a buyer perspective. If you see two items, one has nice clear, well edited photos and the other one has blurry, too dark, or pictures taken from a distance, which one will you click on?

Getting traffic to your listings is extremely important. If you don't get the traffic, your item won't sell for what it should or may not sell at all. Your picture has to draw the shoppers in. You have to get their attention.

You're going to find that for most items listed for sale on eBay or Amazon, there's quite a bit of competition. Unless, of course, your lucky enough to be selling something handmade or rare.

When a perspective buyer does a search on eBay, hundreds of thumbnail pictures can appear on the search results page.

Your goal is to get a perspective buyer to click on your item listing, not your competitions. As they scan through the multiple thumbnails on the search page, your photo needs to be the one to grab their attention. It needs to "pop".

When using a stock photo provided by your supplier, you'll need to change it somehow to make it standout. You can accomplish this by changing the color of the background, or repositioning the item within the photo, maybe cropping it, so the image fills the entire frame.

Your objective is to make your photo stand out from all the other stock photos thumbnails which show when the buyer searches for an item. Chances are good many sellers are using the same supplier, therefore, they're using the same photos. Even if you take your own photos and aren't using stock photos, there may be several other sellers listing the very same item.

Taking and editing photos is a very important aspect to online selling and needs to be done correctly. You can write the best sales copy possible for your item, but if no one clicks into your listing to read it, it won't make a bit of difference. You have to get their attention and make them want to check out what you're selling. Think like a buyer.

The thumbnail in the search results is going to be the first thing they'll see. Your photo needs to give them the desire to look further

Why do I need Good Photos?

People are naturally very visual, especially when they want to purchase an item. Your pictures are a very important part of your online listings. What I've found is that many of my customers have bought items without even reading the description. They've made their purchases solely by looking at the photo, with the growing use of Smartphone's and tablets, this is even more prevalent.

When someone views your listing, they aren't able to touch the item you're trying to sell, or turn it to see different angles. Therefore, they'll have to rely 100% on your photo's to present a clear view of the item. They don't want to spend their money, if they don't know what they're getting. It's always a good idea to have photos from several angles, if possible.

You don't have to be a talented photographer to take great pictures for eBay, or any online site. What you will need to do is put some effort into learning how your camera works and how to work with lighting. You'll also need to practice taking and editing photos.

Fortunately, with the invention of digital cameras, you don't have to pay for photo processing anymore. All you have to do is delete any pictures that don't look exactly the way you want. So just click away and get lots of practice. The more practice you get using your cameras features and editing photos, the more it'll pay off in the end.

Remember, great photos will help to sell your item for top dollar. Take pictures of your item from several angels. Well lit, clear, close up photos are your objective.

Clear and clutter free photos will, without a doubt, bring more perspective buyers to your listing. It's very rare for the first person who looks at your listing to buy your item, so you need lots and lots of lookers.

Don't settle for a mediocre photo, thinking it's "good enough". It isn't. With just a little practice and preparation, anyone can take great pictures. You can acquire this skill faster than you may think.

The more professional looking your photos are, the better. Spend the extra time, your bank account will thank you!

Buying a Digital Camera

With hundreds of digital cameras on the market and more coming out constantly, you may be overwhelmed when you try to select the "right" camera. Anymore, even an inexpensive digital camera will produce wonderful results.

Digital cameras come in many sizes, shapes and price ranges. Most likely you'll be using this camera for a few years, therefore it's a good idea to consider the various options available before making your purchase.

Although cameras come in many sizes, a compact camera is by far the most popular. This camera is the best value for the average user. They normally have quite good picture quality and a nice selection of features.

You don't need an expensive digital camera to take good photos. You may not even need a new one at all. The camera I use right now is several years old and only has 4 Mega pixels. But it still works great, even for close-up details.

If you already own a digital camera, practice taking pictures with it and see how they look. Check the close-up shots for good detail. If everything looks fine, then save yourself some money and use the camera you have.

However, if you are planning to purchase a new digital camera, you may want to check for the following features and determine which ones are important to you.

Low-Resolution or Email Setting – This refers to the size of the photo. This setting is on most digital cameras, so you shouldn't have any problem finding one with this feature.

You would use this setting if you were taking a picture that you were sure you wouldn't need to crop. Cropping will cause you to lose detail. If your photo requires a lot of detail, such as jewelry, you'll need to shoot at 1 or 2 mega pixels and then crop or resize to the desired pixels.

In order for buyer to use eBay's zoom and enlarge function when looking at your photo, the Medium or High file size setting on your camera should be chosen. This gives you a large enough image to accommodate zoom and enlarge.

eBay picture hosting services can handle up to 7 MB image.

Macro Setting – Macro Photography is the term used when describing the ability to focus very close on a small object. Using the macro feature will allow you to focus as close as 3 or 4 inches from the item, sometimes even closer. This is important when photographing small objects or detail.

This function works perfectly when trying to get close-up details, such as the original manufacturer's price tag, jewelry details or the maker's mark on pottery or silver. It's also great to use when you're trying to show the weave or detail of a fabric.

White Balance Adjustment – You use this function when adjusting a camera to account for different color temperatures of light. Almost all cameras have an automatic white balance, however you'll want to make sure the camera you choose allows you to manually select the white balance between fluorescent, incandescent and daylight. Auto White Balance (AWB) compensates for these differences, creating a neutral or "daylight" photo

Manual Focus – The auto focus on digital cameras can often be fooled. It may try to focus on an item other than what you intend. The ability to manually focus on an object, or part of an object, can be very important.

As true as this is, it needs to be said that normally, for eBay pictures, auto focus will work just fine. Your object should fill the frame, so no other item is in the view of the camera to confuse the auto focus.

Exposure Adjustment – The light meter on a camera, like the auto focus feature, can focus improperly when using a bright background. This is especially important if you're using a lighting tent to stage your photos.

Lighting tents often use a white background and can throw off the light meter in a camera. My personal preference is to avoid a stark white background, off white or beige works very well.

Optical Zoom – Digital cameras come with either an optical zoom or a digital zoom. A digital zoom can be very restrictive and difficult to work with when trying to take photo's for auction sites.

Make sure your camera features a basic optical zoom. It's very easy to tell which type of zoom the camera has simply by pushing the zoom button to see if the lens actually moves in and out. If you don't see the lens physically moving, then the camera has a digital zoom feature.

Aperture Priority Setting- This refers to the ability to select a small lens opening (aperture), which allows you to achieve what is referred to as depth of field. This means that objects close to you and far away are both in focus.

Many digital cameras will have a manual aperture setting. Lens openings are marked as a series of numbers that range from 3.5 to 16. The higher the number the more depth of field you'll have. Because the Macro setting (used for close-ups) limits the depth of field, this feature may be important. With close-up photography, a setting of 8 or higher is best. (This is where you'd most likely need a tripod)

USB Connection – Most new cameras will have this cord. Although you can use the camera's memory card to access your photos, using a USB cord is the easiest and fastest way to get your pictures onto your computer. You simply plug your camera into your computer.

Using the cord will allow you to take the pictures directly off your camera and into your photo-editing program or move them into a folder on your computer.

Many laptops don't even have a place for a memory card to plug in, however any computer with USB ports will accept this cord. This gives you a lot of flexibility, as you can look at your pictures on anyone's computer.

Mega Pixels – You may think the more mega pixels, the better, but this is not necessarily the case. A mega pixel is a measure of the quantity (amount of data captured), not the quality. The size of the actual pixels is more important than the number of pixels.

The bigger the pixel size, the better they can record detail in shadows and highlights. Larger sensors generally produce greater dynamic range, better signal-to-noise ratio, and higher sensitivity; this is mostly due to the fact that they have room for bigger, more light-sensitive pixels.

Ask the salesperson about picture quality when comparing cameras; don't just look at pixel count.

LCD – Choose a camera with a bright LCD. This will allow you to better see the LCD image in bright sunlight. Also, having a large LCD screen will help you to compose and review your images on the camera.

Tripod – Not essential, but really nice to have at times. Nearly all cameras will have a standard tripod screw mount located on the bottom of the camera.

A tripod can come in very handy if you're taking photos in dim light or if you're having trouble keeping your hands from shaking. Even the slightest movement can cause your pictures to be blurry.

If you plan to take a lot of close-up photos, it's a good idea to use a tripod. This is especially important when taking pictures of jewelry items. Jewelry items require that your pictures show a lot of clear detail. A steady camera will save you a lot of time by producing clear pictures the first time around.

Most new cameras have an Image Stabilizer button, which will help quite a bit to keep your photos from becoming blurred. But even using this function, you can still produce blurred photos.

Your tripod will need to be sturdy and be adjustable to rotate both vertically and horizontally. Most tripods will have these functions, but it's wise to check it out first, just to be sure.

When you're shopping for a tripod, remember, it doesn't need to be expensive, digital cameras are pretty lightweight. Because the cameras are so lightweight, even inexpensive tripods will work just fine.

Types of Photo Staging Areas

After you've purchased your camera, and possibly a tripod, you'll need to have a photo staging area. This can be accomplished by several methods. You don't need to spend a lot of money to create the prefect setting.

Here are a few ideas for you. Just pick the method that best fits your budget and needs.

Photography Backdrops – You'll find several types and sizes of photography backgrounds/backdrops simply by doing a search on eBay, Amazon, or any search engine, for "Photography Backdrops". A backdrop will work well for larger items. However this could be an expensive way to go. Backdrops on eBay can range from $19.99 to nearly $200.

Photo Cube – These are really nice and come in several sizes. They may also come with a number of options, from different background colors, to a tripod and lighting accessories. Again, you can do a search on eBay, or other online sites, for "Photo Cube" to see what's being offered.

Photo Cubes work great when photographing small, detailed items. They allow for defused lighting, which reduces glare, making taking photos of highly glossed, items much easier.

I've seen these offered anywhere from $29.50 to well over $100.

Photo Tent (or Studio) – Like the Photo Cube, these come in different sizes and can include lighting accessories. A Photo Tent is larger than a cube, however on eBay, sellers use both the term tent and cube, so you'll need to do a search using both terms in order to look through everything. This way you can see what might fit your needs best. A Photo Tent (or Studio) can be quite costly. Some are as much as $500.

Homemade – Now, this is my favorite! Nearly anyone can make something up that will work just fine for them. You aren't going to get the perfect lighting you would have with a cube or tent, but if you're on a budget, you can adjust for this and still get great looking photos.

Building your own photo staging area can be both inexpensive and fun. You should be able to get everything you need for under $25.

With a little experimenting, you can come up with something that works perfectly for your needs.

Building Your Own Photo Staging Area

Building your own Photo Staging Area can save you a lot of money. If you need to stay within a certain budget, this is the perfect way to go.

If you can set up a staging area and leave it, that's the perfect solution. But not everyone has this ability, so the following suggestions can be left in-place or made portable.

The following information will give you suggestions on how to build your own photo staging area.

Building a Backdrop

First, you'll need some type of backdrop. Fabric works great for this.

You can purchase a couple of inexpensive fabric remnants at a fabric store, or on an auction site. There's usually a wide selection of fabric to choose from, regardless of where you decide to make your purchase.

It's best to use a solid color; you don't want to detract from your item by using something with a pattern or design. I use two remnants; one is a solid very pale blue and the other a solid dark blue.

I use the pale blue instead of white, to cut down on the reflective nature of pure white. It's best to have at least two colors, because you'll need to have a contrasting background for the different types of objects your photographing.

You can use as many solid colors as you like. Maybe you'll want to use a certain color for some items and a different color for other items. An example of this would be if you sold jewelry, you might want one color to use for all your necklaces, but a different color when photographing your earrings, and yet another color for bracelets. It's your photo studio; you can create it to suite your needs and personality.

Because I hate ironing, the fabric I chose was a cotton polyester blend, to reduce wrinkles. If your fabric wrinkles easily, you're going to have to iron it before you can use it and that just sounds like work to me.

Wrinkles in your fabric backdrop will really show up in the finished product. It won't look very professional. If you fabric wrinkles, iron it before you use it as a backdrop.

You may also want to be sure your fabric doesn't have a lot of texture to it. When you take close-up photos, textures can be very pronounced and distracting. You're going to want to show the details of your item, not the details of the fabric that you're using as a backdrop.

In addition, be sure the remnant is large enough. The smallest fabric remnant I use is 45" wide by 67" long. I wouldn't go smaller than that, unless you'll only be photographing jewelry or other very small items. You're going to be using this piece of fabric to place your item on and as the backdrop.

Staging Area

The next thing you'll need is something to place your fabric over. You can use a small table or even a couple of cardboard boxes. Because many items will be photographed from several angles, you'll probably want to put them up on a box or short table, so you don't have to lie on the floor to get at eye level.

For very small items, simply drape your fabric over the table or a box. You may need to iron it first, if it has a lot of wrinkles. Winkles look terrible in a picture; it's amazing how well they show up in the final photo!

When photographing very small items, you can take your picture from above or from an angle, at about eye level, but always get as close as you can and use the Macro setting on your camera (usually denoted by a little flower on most camera settings).

Larger items will require a little more effort. You'll need another larger box, a tray table, or something that allows you to drape your fabric over the small box and up onto the larger box or table. This way you'll have a flat surface covered with your fabric with more fabric being used as a backdrop. This gives you a continuous background in the picture of one solid color.

Personally, I simply drape a piece of solid colored cloth over a medium size box, and then up over a TV tray. If

I'm photographing wide items, I have to use a larger box and two trays. Very simple, but effective.

This method allows me to have a small photo booth type set up. This easy arrangement gives me a solid backdrop that doesn't detract from the item. It also prevents any distracting surroundings, like my sofa, kitchen or bookcases, from finding their way into my final photo.

For larger items, I spread my fabric on the floor or on a large box and attach it to the wall. I then place my item on the box or floor, on top of the cloth. This technique allows for the background to be one solid color, making your item the focal point of the photo.

Lighting

Your lighting is a very important consideration. It's always best to use indirect lighting, normally indirect sunlight is best. So setting up your photo staging area where you're able to get indirect morning and afternoon sunlight is a good idea.

Do your best to avoid shadows. Unless a shadow will optimize the look of the item you're photographing, you definitely don't want it in your picture. Shadows are rarely a positive addition.

Setting up your photo staging area with Northern exposure will allow for optimum lighting conditions. However, other exposures can be used effectively. You'll just have to watch the sun to see what times of day will give you the desired lighting conditions.

An overcast day can offer a perfect indirect lighting environment and produce great looking pictures.

Bright, direct sunlight or a flash will tend to make your item look "washed out" or produces a glare. This won't give you the end result you want.

Some items are so shinny that you can't help but get some glare. Be careful! People will be able to see you in the item. There are several photos circulating the web that were taken and listed on eBay. In these photos, you can see a whole lot more than the item being photographed. Word to the wise, you may want to wear clothing while you're taking your pictures!

You'll probably need to experiment a little with the lighting to get everything just right. You may notice that you can only use the area at certain times during the day. If this is the case, you can easily plan your photo shots for those times.

You'll most likely have other work you can do when the lighting isn't at its best. You can always use this time to research your items or editing other photos you've already taken.

Be creative!

Play with colors, lighting and building the perfect staging area. If you're using boxes to drape your fabric over and set your items on, you may need to experiment with different sizes and heights. You'll want to create something that will allow you to be comfortable while taking your pictures.

You may need to move things around, or change your staging area, in order to optimize lighting. Check out the lighting at different times of the day. Make a mental note of the time of day that the lighting is at its best and plan to take your photos at those times.

It can be fun to experiment with what works best for the type of items you sell. Small items, large items, items of various sizes, what can you set up that will work best for your needs.

Besides saving yourself some money, you'll be creating something that works perfectly for you. Now you can get started taking beautiful, professional looking photos, perfect for online listings.

Mistakes to Avoid When Taking Pictures

Have you seen those terrible photos on eBay? You know the ones; they are too light or too dark, out of focus, even (unbelievably!) sideways. Sometimes there's so much clutter in the photo, you don't even know what item is for sale.

Don't be one of those online sellers who believe the photo isn't important. You couldn't be more mistaken! The old adage "A picture is worth a thousand words" applies doubly to online pictures. When all you have is a photo, it had better be a good one!

If your photos are clear and done well, they'll add professionalism to your online listings. This will help to instill buyer confidence. Remember, you're a stranger. If you photo and listing is sloppy, do you really think the buyer is going to have a good feeling about buying from you?

One thing you should know here is that there are actually eBay/Amazon sellers who look for listings with bad photos (misspellings & bad descriptions, too). They can usually buy these items for a great price and resell them at a profit.

They'll take a new photo, rewrite the description and relist your item. They make the money and you lose out. Some sellers actually make a pretty good income this way!

5 Common Mistakes You'll Want to Avoid.

1. **Distracting Background** - Keep you photo free of distraction. Your item needs to be the main focus of your photo, not your living room, family photos or the clutter on the bookshelf.

   It's best to use a simple background. A piece of solid colored fabric or other solid material will work well. Be sure the color doesn't conflict with the color of your item.

   Don't put a lot of other items (props) in your photo that aren't for sale. Buyers think everything in the photo is part of the listing. By adding unneeded items or items that won't be included in the sale, you confuse the buyer and this could lead to trouble after they've made their purchase.

2. **Too Light or Too Dark** – It's best to take your photos using indirect, natural light. Bright light washes out the color and detail, so direct sunlight or using a flash isn't the best idea. Many times this can be corrected with editing, but not always. You'll want to spend as little time as possible editing your photos, so it's best to start with good lighting.

3. **Out of Focus** – Your photo **MUST** be in focus. This is extremely important. Your photo is going to sell your item. Many buyers won't even bother to look at blurry, out of focus photos. They'll skip your listing altogether and you'll lose a potential sale.

Use the correct setting on your camera and hold it steady when taking the picture. You may need to push your elbow against your body and hold your breath when you snap the picture. This will help you keep the camera steady.

A tripod is always helpful, if you're having trouble keeping the camera steady.

4. **Picture Sideways** – Buyer do not like looking at sideways photos. Align your photo correctly. A sideways photo isn't going to draw attention to your listing. It simply looks unprofessional and many buyers won't even bother looking at your listing. You may get the buyers attention, but not in a positive way.

If you have to take the photo sideways to get the entire item in the frame, then you can rotate your photo during editing. All photo editing software allows you to rotate your photo.

5. **Too Far Away** – Your item shouldn't be a tiny speck somewhere in the picture. Zoom in or crop your photo so that you item fills the frame. If your item is small, you can get very close to it by using the Macro setting on your camera (the

little flower is usually the symbol for this setting on most cameras). All you should be able to see is the item you're selling and a small amount of your background fabric.

It may take a little time to learn to take really good photos, but just like the saying goes, *practice makes perfect!*

Be sure to read the instruction manual that came with your camera. Yes, I know it's a bother and most people don't look at the manual, but take the time. You'll be glad you did.

Experiment with the functions and controls on your camera until you feel comfortable using them. Before you know it, you'll be taking great photos.

Watermarking Your Photos

I must caution you **AGAINST** copying another seller's photos. This is against eBay's policy. Although, it is allowed on Amazon.

In fact, the way Amazon is set up, you can actually create your entire listing using one already on the site. Currently, Amazon does not allow text or watermarking on photos.

Presently, eBay's help page states:

You can't use another member's pictures or descriptions without their permission. If another member is using your images or description, let us know.

The eBay policy currently reads:

eBay members are not allowed to use images—including photos and other pictures—or text they didn't create themselves. Exceptions to this policy would be if they are authorized to do so by the owner, its agent, or the law.

The following exception applies:

You can use images and text descriptions from the eBay product catalog in your listings without violating this policy. The product catalog may include, at our discretion, select seller-generated images or photos from seller listings. Unless the seller opts out of this program, the inclusion of such seller-generated photos in the eBay product catalog and the use of catalog content by eBay sellers in their eBay listings is authorized under the User Agreement.

For more detailed information, see eBay's *Images and text policy* page.

Even though eBay has the above policy against using someone else's photos or description, other sellers still do it all the time.

You've spent all your valuable time creating this great photo of your item, just to have another seller take it and use it in their listing. This can be very upsetting.

I guarantee that at some point, this will happen to you. It's happened to me many times. I've even had times when they've copied my entire listing, photos, text and even my selling policies. It's a strange feeling to be checking out the competition and open up someone else's listing only to find your listing looking back at you!

How do you protect your photos from being stolen by another seller? After all, you've worked hard on these pictures! The simplest way is to add text to your photo.

You'll need to watermark your eBay store name or eBay user name onto the photo. Be sure to place a small part of your watermark over part of the object. I made the mistake, early on, of just putting it at the bottom, only to have other sellers simply crop it out and use my photos.

All photo editing programs should have a text tool. It'll only take a minute to add your eBay user ID or Store Name, so take the time. You may think you have something really unique and no one will copy your photo. Unless it's a one-of-a-kind, handmade item, then there are probably more items, just like yours, out there.

Better safe than sorry. It's a terrible feeling to see someone else using your hard work. You can report them to eBay, but unfortunately, many times nothing happens, so they just continue using your photos, at will.

Don't make your watermark too large or have it cover the entire picture. This detracts from the looks of the picture and makes the item you're selling hard to see.

You may want to choose the option to have eBay watermark your pictures. However, this watermark will appear at the very bottom of the frame, making it easy to be cropped out by another seller.

Policy from eBay for Watermarks:

You can use our camera icon, your eBay user ID, or both, as a watermark on your picture. **Note:** *Watermarks are the only text that can be on your picture. Watermarks can't serve a marketing purpose and shouldn't distract from the image.*

Getting Your Image Ready to Upload

Unless you take a perfect photo every time, some editing will be required. The more practice you get, the better you'll be. The best way to save time is to shoot all your photos at one time. Then you can bring them into your photo-editing program and edit them all at once.

Photo Editing Software– It's important to edit your photos. Some digital cameras come with good photo editing software, some don't. Photoshop works great, but is very costly. If you do a search online for "free photo editing software", you'll find many to choose from. GIMP is free and works well, but there are plenty of others. I'm sure you can find one that will suite your needs and abilities.

Editing Your Photo – Now you'll want to edit your photos. Is your photo a little light or too dark? You can usually correct this by adjusting the levels. Too much background? Crop out everything extra, you want your item to be the main focus and to fill the frame. Add your user id or store name using the text tool.

I've actually created a watermark, so I use this when I'm editing photos.

Image Format – Your photo needs to be in the correct format to post on eBay. JPEG is best for photographs.

According to eBay's Help Page, you can upload pictures in the following formats, JPEG, PNG, TIFF, BMP, GIF.

Image Size – eBay allows for pictures to be a minimum of 1600 pixels on the longest side. Your photo should not be smaller than 500 pixels on the longest side. Larger is better.

If you keep the resolution around 72 the picture will load quickly. Remember, your visitors will only wait around 12 seconds for your page to load. Large pictures with high resolution can take forever to load. A resolution of 72 will keep your file small enough without sacrificing picture quality.

Keep in mind that for close-up photos you'll need to use a high resolution on your camera when shooting the picture. However, be sure to edit it to a resolution of 72, with a pixel size of around 1600, before using it in your listing.

Yes, if you do everything you need to do, it is going to take some time and effort. Even though this may seem like a lot of work, it really isn't once you get started. You basically go in, crop, adjust the level (if too light or too dark), adjust your image size and resolution (if necessary) and add your watermark. If your photo needs more editing than that, then you may want to retake the picture.

When you've done this a few times, you'll be amazed at how quickly you can edit your photos and get on to the next step of actually listing your items on eBay.

The end result is well worth the time spent.

Storing Your Photos on the Web

Most auction sites will allow you to upload your item images directly onto their server. This step is generally pretty simple. You would just upload your picture following the direction on the site.

However, there will be times when you'll need to have your own hosting for your photos. Many websites offer this service for a fee, while others still offer it for free. Again, you can do an Internet search for photo hosting and find many to choose from.

The website I really like is Photobucket. This site still offers a free photo hosting plan, at the time of this writing. It's user friendly and the free service offers plenty of photo hosting. I've been using it for over 6 years and have 100's of photos hosted. I still haven't run out of my "free" allotment.

If you already have a website with hosting, you can host your photos with your own web hosting provider, if you choose. Simply build an image file and upload the photos into that file.

Once you've hosted your photos, you'll need to get the URL specific to that photo.

On Photobucket you just click in the box titled "direct link". This automatically copies the link to your computer clipboard. Now you just paste it where you want your photo to show up and you're done.

With your own hosting, you would need to find the photo in your images folder, click on it and copy the URL in the browser address window. Then paste the photo URL in where you need it.

computer clipboard. Now you just paste it where you want your photo to show up and your done.

With your own hosting, you would need to find the photo in your images folder, click on it and copy the URL in the browser address window. Then paste it in where you need it.

You can use this URL address anywhere on the web where you'd like to have your photo displayed. Add it to a blog, put it into an auction template or even add it to Facebook or other social networking sites.

Most auction sites will have a place for you to paste this link, if you don't want to host your photo on their server or if you need to insert them into a selling template.

More photo hosting sites you may want to check out:

- Picasa

- Flickr

- ImageShack

- Tinypic

- PICTIGER

- PICT.COM

This is just a short list of the numerous website available for hosting photos.

How Many Pictures Will I Need?

Well, that depends on what you're selling. Many items may only need one photo, but more often then not, you'll need one of each view, any defects, maker's mark or manufacturers tag, and close-ups of details.

The more photos you provide, the better. You can now use up to 12 photo for free on eBay. Try to use as many as possible.

Rule of Thumb – What I've used as a rule of thumb is the following; if I walked up to this item in a store, would I pick it up and look at the bottom, top and sides? Would I look for identifying marks? If it's large, would I walk around it? Look inside? Open drawers or doors? If it's a piece of jewelry, would I hold it closer to see the detail? If you would want to see certain parts of the item, then so does your buyer.

Defects – If there are any defects, be sure to get pictures of them. It's better for your buyer to see these **BEFORE** they make the purchase.

Many people really don't care if it has a defect, just let them know upfront. You don't want a buyer to be upset and either leave you negative feedback or want to return it.

Honesty is definitely the best policy. Describe and photograph all defects.

Makers Marks and Manufacturers Labels – These are important to many buyers. You'll need to be sure to take pictures of the labels, tags and makers marks. This will prove to your buyers you actually have the item you've listed and they're getting what they're paying for.

Accessories – Be sure to take pictures of all the accessories. Sometime you can put them altogether in one picture. You may want to take separate pictures of each accessory, if that works better for your purpose.

Clothing – Take a full-length photo of the item, front and back. Then take a close-up of the fabric, tags, and labels. If the piece of clothing has any detail, like special buttons or stitching, get a close-up of that also. Don't forget to take pictures of any defects.

Taking pictures of clothing on mannequins is usually best. If you don't have a mannequin, you can hang the item on a hanger and photograph it against a solid colored wall. Just hang it from a nail or hook. When you edit your photo, you can crop out the nail and part of the hanger.

Taking good photos, at various angles, will enable the buyer to see exactly what they're getting, so there's no surprised when it arrives. You can write a great description, but seeing the photos can make all the difference between a looker and a buyer.

One thing you're going to want to do is take 2 or 3 pictures of each angle. That way chances are good that at least one of them will be good and require very little, if any, editing. You don't want to have to go back, set everything up again and retake your photos. This is a waste of time, not to mention frustrating.

Also, if the clothing is wrinkled, iron it. Wrinkles really show up in a photo. Even if the item is used, a buyer wants it to look new. Clothing should be clean, any small tears should be repaired and item must be pressed, before pictures are taken.

How to Take Photos when Scale is Important

Sometimes the items actual size will be critically important to the buyer; an example of this would be Doll House furniture, model trains, tiny tea sets or any other type of miniatures.

Hobbyists who collect miniatures tend to collect in a single size range, such as 1:25 for dollhouse miniatures, which are available in at least three scales. They're only going to be interested in the size item that will fit into their Doll House, not everything available. It's important that the buyer be able to make the determination as to the scale of the item.

When scale is important, it's best to place a ruler in your photograph for items, such as miniature furniture or tiny appliances. If you're selling something smaller like dishes or a potted plant, place a coin, like a dime, nickel or quarter, in the photo. This will give your buyer a point of reference, so they can make an informed decision on the item size before making the purchase.

Whatever you place in the picture, just remember to mention in the description that it isn't part of the sale. It may seem obvious to you, but don't assume it'll be obvious to everyone. It's essential to avoid any customer disappointment or dissatisfaction, whenever possible.

Another tip you may want to use is to set your camera to its highest resolution. This will give you a better quality picture, showing more detail. But keep in mind when you edit it to change the resolution of 72 before you add it to your listing. Remember, this is the fastest loading resolution.

When photographing detail, you'll need to be very close to the item, so be sure to hold your camera VERY steady. To keep the camera as steady as possible, you may want to hold it with both hands. If possible, hold the camera tight to your chest or another body part, for stability. If you have a tri-pod, now is the time to use it.

Another good idea is to be sure your lens is clean. Smudges will cause your photo to appear out of focus.

What is a Full Disclosure Photo?

Even though I've already mentioned the importance of taking pictures of any item defects, I felt I needed to elaborate more on the subject.

As a new seller or even an experienced one, you never want to disappoint your customers and possibly receive negative feedback, as a result. Even if you have an item a perspective customer really wants, if they see a lot of negative feedback, they'll usually look elsewhere. Your customers want to make a purchase and move on, they don't want any hassles. Also, too many negative feedback and you could lose your selling privileges on eBay or Amazon.

The way to avoid disappointing your customers is to meet or exceed their expectations. You can do this by taking clear photos of any defects your item may have.

Don't think that just because your item has defects, no one will want it. This isn't necessarily the case. Many damaged items are purchased simply to be used for parts or in craft projects. Just remember, there is a market for damaged and inexpensive items.

Don't kid yourself that they won't notice. If you noticed it, so will they. Just tell them about it and show them a picture right upfront. This will save you from enduring a lot of headaches later!

On the other hand, you may want to photograph an item in a way that shows it's working. An example of this would be a television or computer screen, turn it on and take a picture showing that it's in working order.

If a buyer can see your item working in the photo, they'll be reassured that the item they are buying is actually in working condition. Buyer confidence is key to online sales.

Now What?

I can't tell you the number of times I've had someone come to me and ask how to list an item on eBay. Of course, I begin by telling them that the first thing they'll need to do is to take really a few good pictures. Unbelievably, they actually begin explaining to me how the picture isn't really that important, anything sells on eBay.

Well, the truth is, not everything sells on eBay. There are actually some items that no one wants. I agree, some of the things that do sell are quite interesting, to say the least. Sometimes it's amazing what people will actually buy. But junk is junk, and no one wants it.

Pictures **ARE** important! If you've taken a great picture, your item will stand out and possibly get someone's attention. If it looks like junk, they'll think it's junk and not bother clicking on your listing. They'll never read your great description which explains what a gem it actually is.

Selling online is kind of like the honor system. You're perspective customers need to feel as though they can trust you. One way to accomplish this is to look and act as professional as possible. A great method of doing this is by having good photos in your listings.

If you pay attention to your lighting, focus and the centering of your item, you can keep the editing to a minimum. Don't spend a lot of your valuable time editing bad photos. If your photo doesn't look right, pull out your camera and try again.

You'll waste more time trying to edit a bad photo then you will just retaking it. Pay attention to what you didn't like about the photo. When you retake it, just be sure that you don't make the same mistake.

Reminder – take several photos of your item at one time, you're bond to get some good ones and you can delete all the others.

The more practice you get, the quicker the process will become. Time is money, so get your photo staging area set up, practice taking and editing photos, and **Start Selling**!

ABOUT THE AUTHOR

Judy Wesener has been a power seller on eBay since 2006 and is currently a top rated seller. Her eBay user id is thebestgeneralstore.

At the time this book was written, she had sold thousands of items and has taken and/or edited countless photos.

In addition to eBay, she sells on 5 other online sites, including her own website.

She's currently in the process of creating two more eCommerce websites.

Watch for other books from this author.

Glossary of Terms

Ambient light – The natural light in a scene.

Archival – The ability of a material, including some printing papers and compact discs, to last for many years.

Aperture – A small, circular opening inside the lens that can change in diameter to control the amount of light reaching the camera's sensor as a picture is taken. The aperture diameter is expressed in f-stops; the lower the number, the larger the aperture. For instance, the aperture opening when set to f/2.8 is larger than at f/8. The aperture and shutter speed together control the total amount of light reaching the sensor. A larger aperture passes more light through to the sensor. Many cameras have an aperture priority mode that allows you to adjust the aperture to your own liking. See also *shutter speed*.

Application – A computer program, such as an image editor or image browser.

Buffer – Memory in the camera that stores digital photos before they are written to the memory card.

Burning – Selectively darkening part of a photo with an image-editing program.

CCD – Charge Coupled Device: one of the two main types of image sensors used in digital cameras. When a picture is taken, the CCD is struck by light coming through the camera's lens. Each of the thousands or millions of tiny pixels that make up the CCD convert this light into electrons. The number of electrons, usually described as the pixel's accumulated charge, is measured, then converted to a digital value. This last step occurs outside the CCD, in a camera component called an analog-to-digital converter.

CD-R – CD-Recordable: a compact disc that holds either 650 or 700 MB of digital information, including digital photos. Creating one is commonly referred to as *burning a CD*. A CD-R disc can only be written to once, and is an ideal storage medium for original digital photos.

CD-RW – CD-Rewritable: similar in virtually all respects to a CD-R, except that a CD-RW disc can be written and erased many times. This makes them best suited to many backup tasks, but not for long term storage of original digital photos.

CMOS – Complementary Metal-Oxide Semiconductor: one of the two main types of image sensors used in digital cameras. Its basic function is the same as that of a CCD. CMOS sensors are currently found in only a handful of digital cameras.

CMYK – Cyan, Magenta, Yellow, Black. The four colors in the inksets of many photo-quality printers. Some printers use six ink colors to achieve smoother, more photographic prints. The two additional colors are often lighter shades of cyan and magenta.

CompactFlash™ – A common type of digital camera memory card, about the size of a matchbook. There are two types of cards, Type I and Type II. They vary only in their thickness, with Type I being slightly thinner. A

CompactFlash memory card can contain either flash memory or a miniature hard drive. The flash memory type is more prevalent.

Contrast – The difference between the darkest and lightest areas in a photo. The greater the difference, the higher the contrast.

Depth of field – Indicates how much of a scene will be sharp and in focus. A greater depth of field implies an increased distance between well-focused background and foreground, with everything in between properly focused. A narrow depth of field concentrates the area of sharp focus within a small range, based on the main subject's distance from the camera.

For instance, if your subject is standing in an open field, using a narrow depth of field will make most of the scene in front and behind look blurry; only the main subject will be focused. This effect is achieved when using long zoom lens. Using a wide-angle lens will produce a greater depth of field, thereby keeping the whole scene in focus.

Digital camera – A camera that captures the photo not on film, but in an electronic imaging sensor that takes the place of film.

Dodging – Selectively lightening part of a photo with an image-editing program.

Compression – A process that reduces the amount of data representing an image so that the file takes up less space in your camera, memory card, or computer. Smaller files are quicker to use for e-mail and on the

Web. When a file is too compressed, however, image quality can seriously suffer.

Download, downloading – The process of moving computer data from one location to another. Though the term is normally used to describe the transfer, or downloading, of data from the Internet, it is also used to describe the transfer of photos from a camera memory card to the computer. *Example: I downloaded photos to my PC.*

DPI – Dots per inch: A measurement of the resolution of a digital photo or digital device, including digital cameras and printers. The higher the number, the greater the resolution.

Compression – A process that reduces the amount of data representing an image so that the file takes up less space in your camera, memory card, or computer. Smaller files are quicker to use for e-mail and on the Web. When a file is too compressed, however, image quality can seriously suffer.

EXIF – Exchangeable Image File: the file format used by most digital cameras. For example, when a typical camera is set to record a JPEG, it's actually recording an EXIF file that uses JPEG compression to compress the photo data within the file.

External flash – A supplementary flash unit that connects to the camera with a cable, or is triggered by the light from the camera's internal flash. Many fun and creative effects can be created with external flash.

File – A computer document.

Fill flash – A flash technique used to brighten deep shadow areas, typically outdoors on sunny days. Some digital cameras include a fill flash mode that forces the flash to fire, even in bright light.

Fire – Slang for shooting a picture. *Example: I pressed the shutter button to fire.*

FireWire – A type of cabling technology for transferring data to and from digital devices at high speed. Some professional digital cameras and memory card readers connect to the computer over FireWire. FireWire card readers are typically faster than those that connect via USB. Also known as IEEE 1394, FireWire was invented by Apple Computer but is now commonly used with Windows-based PCs as well.

Grayscale – A photo made up of varying tones of black and white. Grayscale is synonymous with black and white.

Highlights – The brightest parts of a photo.

Histogram – A graphic representation of the range of tones from dark to light in a photo. Some digital cameras include a histogram feature that enables a precise check on the exposure of the photo.

Image browser – An application that enables you to view digital photos. Some browsers also allow you to rename files, convert photos from one file format to another, add text descriptions, and more.

Image editor – A computer program that enables you to adjust a photo to improve its appearance. With image editing software, you can darken or lighten a photo, rotate it, adjust its contrast, crop out extraneous detail, remove red-eye and more.

Image resolution - The number of pixels in a digital photo is commonly referred to as its image resolution.

Image sensor – The semiconductor chip or Image Sensor is what captures the photographic image. It collects the light of a scene or subject, which it turns into digital data that we see as a photo in the camera or on the computer. There are two main types of image sensors CCD (charge-coupled device) and CMOS (complementary metal-oxide semiconductor). The CCD is the most popular. CMOS is used in very low and high-end cameras.

Inkjet – A printer that places ink on the paper by spraying droplets through tiny nozzles.

Interpolation – A process that increases image file size and can take place either in the camera or by computer software. Interpolation is used to magnify a picture but does not improve image quality and in fact it can decrease sharpness

ISO speed – A rating of a film's sensitivity to light. Though digital cameras don't use film, they have adopted the same rating system for describing the sensitivity of the camera's imaging sensor. Digital cameras often include a control for adjusting the ISO speed; some will adjust it automatically depending on the lighting conditions, adjusting it upwards as the available light dims. Generally, as ISO speed climbs, image quality drops.

JPEG – A standard for compressing image data developed by the Joint Photographic Experts Group, hence the name JPEG. Strictly speaking, JPEG is not a file format; it's a compression method that is used within a file format, such as the EXIF-JPEG format common to digital cameras. It is referred to as a lossy format, which means some quality is lost in achieving JPEG's high compression rates. Usually, if a high-quality, low-compression JPEG setting is chosen on a digital camera, the loss of quality is not detectable to the eye.

LCD – Liquid Crystal Display: a low-power monitor often used on the top and/or rear of a digital camera to display settings or the photo itself. A small screen on the back of a camera that displays what the lens sees. It is used to compose the picture, choose settings, focus and frame an image in macro mode. It is also used to view photos stored on the memory card.

Media – Material that information is written to and stored on. Digital photography storage media includes CompactFlash cards and CDs.

Megabyte (MB) – A measurement of data storage equal to 1024 kilobytes (KB).

Megapixel – Equal to one million pixels. A measure of a digital camera's resolution. A three-mega pixel rating means that the camera can capture up to 3 million pixels, or points of data.

Memory Card - A removable storage device that holds the images a digital camera captures. It is a good idea to have an extra one on hand so that when one card is full it can be swapped for another allowing you to continue shooting.

Memory Stick®—A memory card slightly smaller than a single stick of chewing gum. Like CompactFlash and SmartMedia, it is flash-based storage for your photos. A removable storage device that holds the images a digital camera captures.

NiMH – Nickel Metal-Hydride: a type of rechargeable battery that can be recharged many times. NiMH batteries provide sufficient power to run digital cameras and flashes.

Online photo printer – A company that receives digital photos uploaded to its Web site, prints them, then sends the prints back by mail or courier.

Panning – A photography technique in which the camera follows a moving subject. Done correctly, the subject is sharp and clear, while the background is blurred, giving a sense of motion to the photo.

Pixel – Picture Element: digital photographs are comprised of thousands or millions of them; they are the building blocks of a digital photo. A point of data in a digital image; the word is short for picture element. A digital camera's resolution is a measure of the number of pixels it can capture on its image sensor.

RAW – The RAW image format is the data as it comes directly off the CCD, with no in-camera processing is performed.

Red-eye – The red glow from a subject's eyes caused by light from a flash reflecting off the blood vessels behind the retina in the eye. The effect is most common when light levels are low, outdoor at night, or indoor in a dimly-lit room.

RGB – Red, Green, Blue: the three colors to which the human visual system, digital cameras and many other devices are sensitive.

Saturation – How rich the colors are in a photo.

Sensitivity – See *ISO speed*.

Sharpness – The clarity of detail in a photo.

Shutter speed – The camera's shutter speed is a measurement of how long its shutter remains open as the picture is taken. The slower the shutter speed, the longer the exposure time. When the shutter speed is set to 1/125 or simply 125, this means that the shutter will be open for exactly 1/125th of one second. The shutter speed and aperture together control the total amount of light reaching the sensor. Some digital cameras have a shutter priority mode that allows you to set the shutter speed to your liking. See also *aperture*.

SmartMedia™—a wafer-thin, matchbook size memory card. This is also a flash-memory based storage medium.

Thumbnail – A small version of a photo. Image browsers commonly display thumbnails of photos several or even dozens at a time. In Windows XP's My

Pictures, you can view thumbnails of photos in both the Thumbnails and Filmstrip view modes.

USB – Universal Serial Bus: a protocol for transferring data to and from digital devices. Many digital cameras and memory card readers connect to the USB port on a computer. USB card readers are typically faster than cameras or readers that connect to the serial port, but slower than those that connect via FireWire.

White Balance – A function on the camera to compensate for different colors of light being emitted by different light sources.